A BRIEF

For centuries a road has run along the coast connecting Shoreham and Brighton. Today it is the A259, once it was little more than a track, which in Southwick and Fishersgate ran under the cliff. This road was affected by coastal erosion and the constant movement of the River Adur. In 1781 this problem was overcome by the building of a turnpike road on the cliff top. (Ironically the "new" road was endangered 180 years later when a large part of the cliff slipped into the canal east of the Schooner.) This new road was better suited to the wheeled traffic and faster travel needed in a time of expansion. Brighton had begun its rapid growth and was a magnet for trade whilst soon the outbreak of war with revolutionary France would bring large numbers of troops to be stationed along the coast, temporarily increasing traffic and trade. At this time Southwick was a small, largely agricultural village, centred on the Green with the river Adur flowing past it to an outlet at Aldrington. The present beach was legally a part of the parish of Lancing and was not joined to Southwick.

Pubs and maltings

The new road brought more people through the village and new buildings began to spring up along it, to serve travellers and for the convenience of local people. One of the early buildings may have been the Victory Inn (the battle of Trafalgar was in 1805). By 1835 The Schooner Hotel had actually been built on the cliff side with entrances from both roads. In 1816 a new harbour entrance was established at Kingston and in the same year John Vallance built a new maltings behind the Schooner. Vallance lived in the Manor House in Hove Street, Hove, and would have found the turnpike a quick and convenient route by which to reach his new investment.

The spot for oysters

The end of the French war in 1815 had brought the prospect of more and safer trade and the port was beginning to grow with new wharves and ship yards. The turnpike road was ideally placed to serve the increasing population of harbour workers and traders and also brought visitors on outings from Brighton to sample the oysters which were raised in huge numbers in Southwick. A favourite venue to buy oysters was the hulk of an old ship called Albion, this was beached on the old road near the present Albion public house. By 1841 this fashionable spot had led to the naming of Albion Street, which by now was home to over 300 people. A little to the west stood a small house which became known as the Crab Cottage, its ruins can still be seen. The oyster beds themselves were south of Albion Street on the site now occupied by Turberville Wharf. They were owned by the Brazier family who established an oyster bar in Brighton (now English's), their name can still be seen on the brass plates outside the restaurant.

Robert Penney - shipowner

The largest house stood at the corner of Albion Street and what is now Grange Road but was then only a path leading from the Green. It was the home of Edward Lucas, a local corn and coal merchant who also owned six small sailing ships. In 1852 he handed over the business to his son in law, Robert Penney who developed the firm into a thriving shipping line trading as far away as New Zealand. His wharf was on the south side of Albion Street and he built warehouses and a sail loft behind his home which he named Alicandu. When Penney left, the house became a school known as The Grange and eventually gave this name to the road.

Railways and a canal

Construction of the railway line, completed in 1840, physically separated Albion Street and it became a densely populated commercial and industrial area with a character quite distinct from rural Southwick. Many of the new buildings would have been built with bricks made locally in the Brickground east of Kingston Lane and the Rock Brickyard near the station (Butts Meadow).

20th February 1855 saw the opening of the Canal and its lock (now the dry dock). The first ship through was the 158 ton brig George, she had been built at Kingston in 1839 and spent her career bringing coal to the port. The new canal encouraged more trade and development, such as the gasworks built just over the border in Portslade in 1871. Thirty years later Brighton Corporation built Southwick's first power station; its second was started in 1947, of which only a lone chimney remains today. Together the gasworks and power stations employed large numbers of local people and brought an enormous trade in coal to the harbour. Indeed latterly the need to provide facilities for bigger coal ships led to the modernisation of the port.

Sailing ships and yachts

In 1862 John Shuttleworth established a ship yard at the bottom of Southwick Street where he built wooden sailing ships such as Capella (246 tons) and Arcturus (279 tons) both of which were owned by Robert Penney. Shuttleworth died tragically young and his yard was not suited to building the iron ships then coming into vogue. It passed instead to Courtney and Birkett who built and maintained yachts. The area is now the Lady Bee Marina but some of the old workshops survive as a chandlery and restaurant.

One of the most famous yachts to be based in Southwick was the large and luxurious Sunbeam owned by Earl Brassey, son of the millionaire railway-builder Thomas Brassey. He used Sunbeam extensively for world-wide travel often on Government business. Most famous was his circumnavigation of the world in 1876/7, the first for a vessel like Sunbeam. His wife, Annie, published an account of this voyage, A Voyage in the Sunbeam, which became an instant best seller. Whilst Annie was sailing the world, Clara Butt, daughter of a sea captain, was born in a small terraced house opposite Brazier's oyster beds. She was christened at the Methodist Church in a huge sea shell brought home by Captain T. Glazebrook, master of Robert Penney's barque, Cora Linn. Clara became one of Britain's greatest singers, a Dame of the British Empire and was especially well known for her singing of "Land of Hope and Glory".

New buildings

Shops, offices, workshops and pubs were attracted to this new population centre and in turn attracted more people. The pub names often give clues to their age and local occupations. (The Victory Inn, the Battle of Trafalgar was in 1805, The Railway Tavern, after the railway which arrived in 1840, Sir Robert Napier after the general who became a national hero after a successful campaign in Abyssinia in 1868, The Shipwrights' Arms and The Sawyers' Arms, recalling shipbuilding trades, and The Mariners' Arms and The Sea House, no doubt both hoping to attract seamen.)

In 1865 Charles Cabot opened the first Post Office in Southwick, in Albion Street near Lock Road. Next door was Charles Ward's shop, he had come from London and doubled as chemist and dentist. Across the road A. O. Muggeridge had already in 1853 established his ships chandlery, the firm still trades in Shoreham and his store still stands next to the Port Offices. In 1873 Waters' Stores opened on the corner of Albion Street and Lock Road, this shop was to sell groceries for nearly a century.

By 1876 the Methodists had moved from their original meeting place in Penney's grain store to a new church opposite the ship yard. Next door was the depot for the trams running between Shoreham and Aldrington (1884-1912). The 1880s also saw the building of a new Coastguard Station (still standing), which by 1891 was home for 51 people.

When Southwick became an Urban District with its own Council in 1899 civic pride and practicality soon led to the building of a new Town Hall (1906) on the field where George Rome had kept his dairy cattle. This replaced a small shared office in a single storey building behind the Grange.

The First World War

During the First World War the army took over the Green to provide a camp for some of the huge numbers of troops being trained in the area. In 1916 they were displaced by men employed building what became known as the "Mystery Towers". These were huge, hollow concrete towers designed to be towed into the English Channel where they would be sunk to form part of an anti-submarine defence system. Work started in the channel south of the Canal, (this was known locally as the South Gut) roughly opposite the Coastguard Station and involved the destruction of the Jubilee Bridge to form a dam. These towers were never finished and work started on others in the outer harbour opposite Kingston Lane. Huge quantities of materials were needed and a railway was built across Albion Street and the Lock to carry them from the main coast line to the work site on the beach. Only one tower was ever completed and now forms the Nab Tower off the Isle of Wight. After the war rubble from the demolished tower was used to fill in Brazier's oyster beds to form Turberville Wharf.

The Second World War

The inter-war years of this century saw the building of more wharves, another lock into the Canal and expansion of the power station. At the same time Southwick was joined to Fishersgate by the houses in The Gardens and Seaview Estate. In 1940 the harbour was largely taken over by the armed forces and Albion Street became a restricted area. There were road blocks at each end, gun emplacements on the Canal bank and passes were needed by people entering the street by one of the check points.

Redevelopment

After the war the Council began to plan a redevelopment programme to provide modern homes and shopping facilities away from the traffic of the busy main road, this coincided with massive modernisation of the harbour facilities. In the 1960s a new shopping centre was opened in Southwick Square and almost all the buildings in Albion Street and Butts Road were demolished and two side roads, Lock Road and Rock Road disappeared entirely. Courtney and Birkett's great timber sail loft next to the Town Hall refused to go quietly and instead burned down in a spectacular blaze. Today only a handful of the original buildings, including; The Schooner, the old Coastguard Station, The Sussex Yacht Club, The old Town Hall, Barnes' chandlery, Muggeridge's store and the flint buildings on Half Tide Quay, remain to remind us of the old community of Albion Street.

1. An aerial view of Albion Street and the harbour looking west, c1934. The "Prince George" lock has recently been opened but the beach has not yet been developed. The Canal tow path can be seen in the centre of the picture.

2. Below the cliff at Fishersgate where the Brighton road once ran. The building on the left was a maltings which stood behind the Fishersgate Coastguard Station. The gasworks was opened just across the Portslade border in 1871.

3. Southwick Power Station was built by Brighton Corporation. Opened on 16th June 1906, it generated electricity until 1976. The chimneys were blown up on 12th June 1977. The houses in Fishersgate and the chimney of Flinn's Dyeworks can be seen on the left.

4. Ester Hall, who sold the land, imposed strict conditions on the appearance of the impressive 1880s Coastguard Station built to replace the one at Fishersgate. The new Brighton "B" Power Station (1947-52) blocked the view of the sea and the station was replaced by a new one at Soldiers' Point, Shoreham.

5. The "Jubilee Bridge" built to connect Southwick with the beach. Its name commemorates the jubilee of Queen Victoria It had a short life being converted into a dam in the First World War. The building of the "Prince Philip Lock" and new wharves in the 1950s made it redundant.

6. The maltings built by John Vallance in 1816. These buildings, now used by the Sussex Yacht Club, still stand behind the Town Hall. The Vallances were part owners of Brighton's "West Street Brewery".

7. The Town Hall built by Southwick Council in 1906. The Council Chamber was on the first floor and Barclay's Bank had a branch in the ground floor of the tower. Towards the end of its life, in the 1970s, the Council concentrated all its offices at Southwick's Manor House.

8. Southwick Council and its officers shortly after the opening of the Town Hall. The man wearing a top hat, second from the right in the middle row, is George Albert Smith, an important pioneer of cinemaphotography and colour film. His home and laboratory were in Roman Crescent.

9 & 10. *"Twitzer" Bennett lived opposite the Town Hall in Norfolk Terrace. She complained vociferously about the noise of the chimes in the clock tower and persuaded the Council to silence them. Members of her family kept a fishmonger's in Grange Road and a builders merchant's yard in Park Lane.*

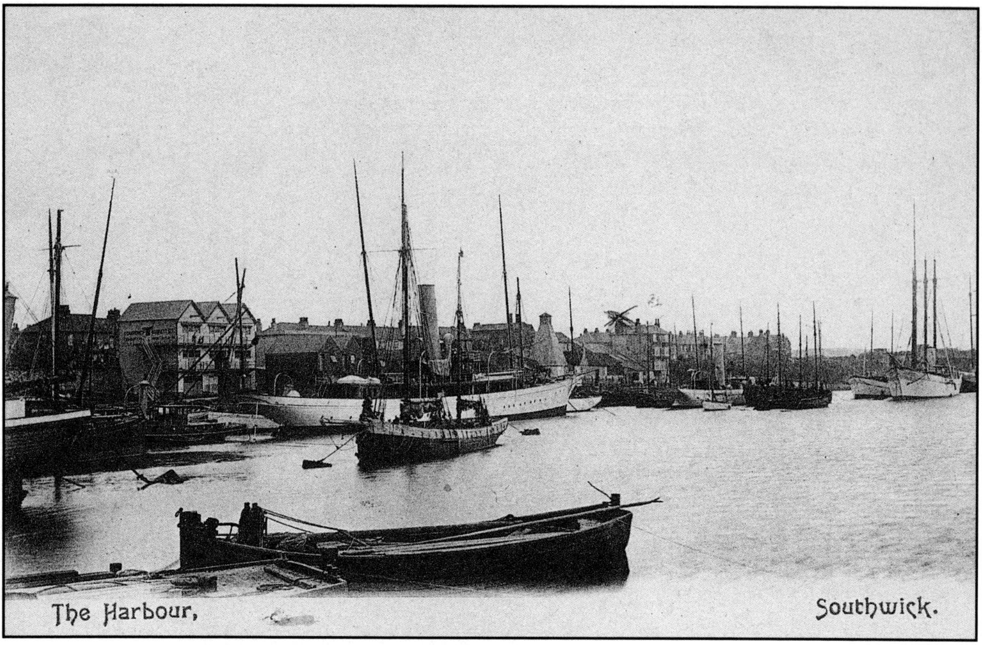

The Harbour, Southwick.

11 & 12. Lily Bennett lived at 13, Norfolk Terrace and sent this card to her friend Emmie in 1906, she marked her home with a cross. At this time postcards were widely used to send everyday messages of all sorts.

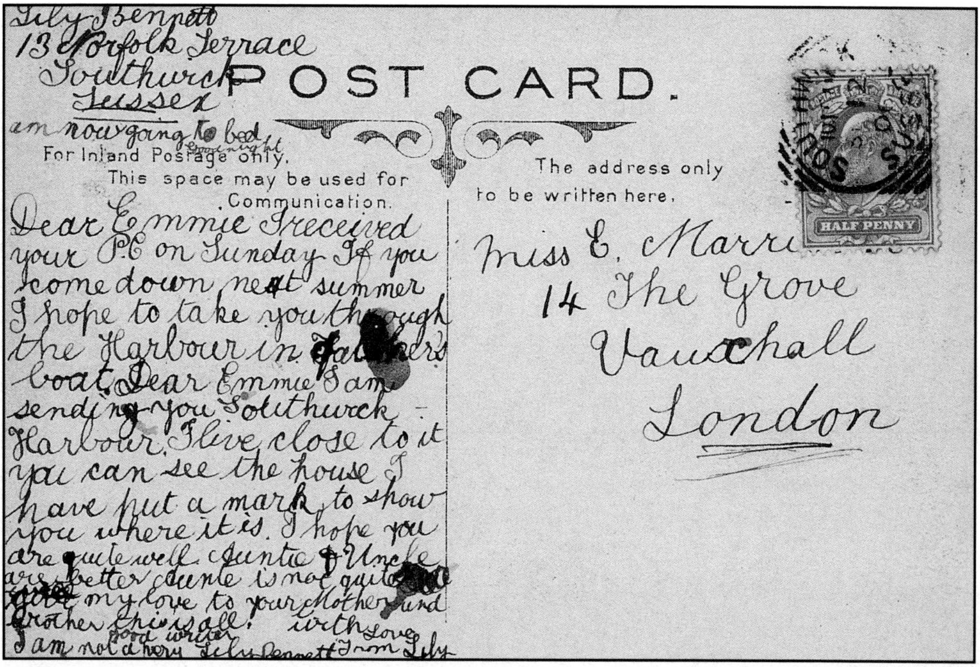

Earl Brassey's Famous Yacht „Sunbeam" which has traversed round the world

13. Southwick was a base for luxury yachts like the "Sunbeam" in which Earl Brassey circumnavigated the world in 1876/7. Many local men crewed these vessels and Courtney and Birckett did a lot of work maintaining them.

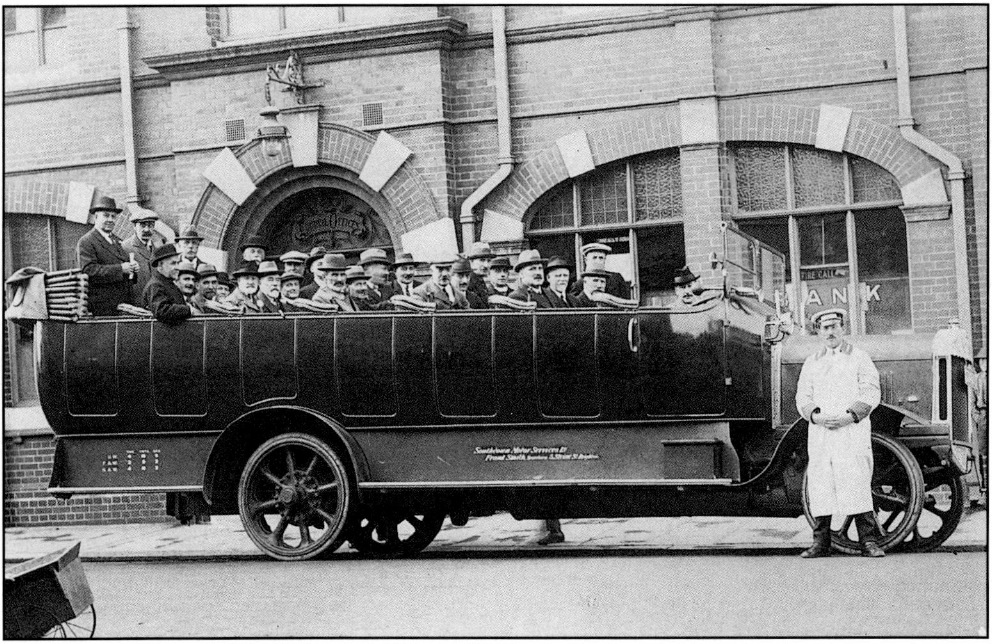

14. In the 1920s open-topped Southdown charabancs were used for local outings, this one is outside the Town Hall and the passengers are believed to include local councillors and officers.

15. Southwick's Annual Regatta attracted huge crowds like this one near the Schooner in 1912. The calm sheltered waters of the Canal were ideal for racing and the Sussex Yacht Club was founded here in 1892.

16. Courtney and Birkett's boatyard was under the cliff west of the Town Hall; as well as building and fitting out yachts the firm undertook general engineering work such as the steep-grade railway at Devil's Dyke. This c1920 view shows the Methodist church in the background.

17. Now the "Lady Bee Marina", this yard was established by John Shuttleworth in 1862. During the Second World War it undertook a lot of work on coastal forces craft for the Royal Navy.

18. The appropriately named "Shipwrights' Arms" stood opposite the shipyard on the corner of Rock Road. The name "Rock" or "Rocks" was often used for the area on old maps.

19. *The Methodist Church built in 1876, stood opposite the shipyard, just west of Southwick Street. In the 1950s the congregation moved to Southwick Street and this building was taken over by the Grange Press. The tram depot was in the yard next door behind the fence.*

20. *A horse drawn tram from Shoreham has just passed Lock Road on the left on its way to Aldrington, c1910. Waters' grocery stood on the corner with Cabot's Post Office and china shop and Ward's chemist's shop and dental surgery nearby.*

21. The approach to the lock in about 1934. The building left of Courtney & Birkett's is Peters' bakery. During the Second World War this area was used as a store for "kite" balloons used to protect ships. The Customs house car park now covers some of this land.

22. Opened in 1855, the first lock collapsed in 1907. The yacht "Candice" was in the lock at the time but was pulled out safely. The masts of the Norwegian barque "Siegrid" can be seen in the background, she was able to leave the following day, piloted by Capt. Fred Grant, senior.

23. *Just before the First World War the "Stephenson Clark" collier "Seaford" leaves the Canal. The ships of this line brought millions of tons of coal to the gasworks and the power station over a period of about 70 years. Locally owned, the ships were named after Sussex towns.*

24. *The tanker "Shell Mex 8" entering the new "Prince George Lock" from the Canal. The original lock, which it replaced, became a dry dock. The beach in the background is still totally undeveloped except for the power station at Fishersgate, c1933.*

25. The "Sea House" pub (c1914) stood between Lock Road and Southwick Street. A block of flats with the same name stands near here today. Nearby is "Coates Court" named after the Council's Engineer and Surveyor responsible for the redevelopment of the area.

26. Shops and the former "Railway Tavern" (behind the Garage sign) opposite the Harbour Offices just after the Second World War. The tavern closed before the Second World War and became the offices of Warr and King, a firm of surveyors. George Warr was Southwick Council's surveyor for over 30 years.

27. Ward's Drug Store and Cabot's Post Office at the start of the 20th century. Mrs Cabot also sold china ware. Not long afterwards a new Post Office was established next door but one to the "Commercial" pub which stood on the west corner of Lock Road.

28. This distinguished gentleman is Charles Ward who kept the "Drug Store" next to the Post Office and also provided a dental service for the town. He lived over the shop with his family.

29. "Alicandu" was the big bay windowed house at the corner of Grange Road and was the home of Robert Penney the ship owner, c1870. He lived here with his wife Lucy and their five children. The business originally belonged to her father, Edward Lucas.

30. By the 20th century, after a brief period as a school called the "Grange," the house had become home to a shop, the Higham sisters' printing press and a garage. The Highams' business is the direct ancestor of the Grange Press which today trades from Butts Road.

31. Fire destroyed the store next door before the First World War. Shortly afterwards it became Kempshall's Garage and now, over 70 years later is still trading as the "Central Garage".

32. By 1924 the Highams' press had moved to the former tram depot next to the Methodist Church. This shop had originally been part of the tram depot.

33. Robert Penney built stores and offices behind his house. In 1899 this one, which fronted Albion Street, provided offices for; the Brighton Union Bank, J. Edward Dell, the solicitor, and for the newly established Southwick Urban District Council!

34. An interior view of the cramped offices.

35. Penney's sail loft became a seamen's mission around the turn of the century and later, the offices of the Shoreham Shipping and Coal Company which owned Turberville Wharf opposite.

36. West of Grange Road there was a row of houses called Adur Terrace, today the site is a lorry park. The contralto singer Dame Clara Butt who suggested the words of "Land of Hope and Glory" was born here (or in the nearby Ann's Place) in the 1870s, she was baptised in the Methodist Church.

37 & 38. In 1947 work started on building a new power station. Today, all has been demolished except the west chimney It was the need to bring in large ships to supply coal to the power station which led to the enlargement and modernisation of the harbour facilities in the 1950s.

39. During the First World War these great concrete "Mystery Towers" were built to defend against German submarines. Only one was finished and here is being towed from the harbour after the war. It is now the Nab Light Tower off the Isle of Wight.

40. The hulk of the "Albion" below the cliff roughly opposite the present "Albion" pub. The "Crab Cottage" is in the distance, both became well-known for the sale of shellfish. Local legend has it that a smuggler's tunnel ran north from the Cottage.